THE QUIET BALANCE

Lessons from the Life Behind the Suit

Dr. Ranjeet Bhelke

Verses Kindler Publication

***Verses Kindler Publication*.**

Website: www.verseskindlerpublication.com

The Quiet Balance
By: Dr. Ranjeet Bhelke
ISBN: 978-93-47494-41-3
Cover Concept and Design: Manali Sureshbabu A.
1st Edition
Price: INR 499/$15

Disclaimer

Dr. Ranjeet Bhelke is the author of ***The Quiet Balance***. The entirety of this published work comprises the original content of the author, who has undertaken diligent efforts in its editing. The characters depicted herein may be fictitious or inspired by real events; however, they are not intended to cause offence or represent any prejudice against any caste or system. Any similarity to the names of actual individuals, locations, or institutions is purely coincidental and serves the narrative. The author bears sole responsibility for the originality of this work; the publisher assumes no liability thereof.

Table of Contents

With Gratitude

Before these words became a book, they were conversations, reflections, and silent reckonings — shaped quietly by the presence of those who walked beside me.

No meaningful work is ever created in isolation. This work rests upon the quiet strength, faith, and generosity of those who stood steady while these pages found their form.

To my wife *Sharvari*, my daughter *Rama*, and to *Dad* and *Mummy* — your love, patience, and unwavering presence became the unseen foundation beneath every chapter. In moments of doubt, when failure felt heavier than insight, it was your steady faith that restored courage and clarity.

To *Archu Randhava*, who listened when ideas were still fragile, who questioned with discernment, and who helped transform uncertainty into articulation — your conversations sharpened both thought and intention.

To *Sarang Chitinis*, whose intellectual engagement and meticulous editing and proofreading shaped scattered drafts into coherence — your precision strengthened the integrity of this manuscript.

'The Quiet Balance' was written by my hand,

but it was shaped by your faith,

refined by your insight,

and sustained by your belief.

With deep appreciation and respect,

Yours Ranjeet

Note of Gratitude

Preface

The Truth Behind the Suit

Hi, I'm Dr. Ranjeet Bhelke.

I wasn't born into comfort.

My childhood began in a cramped *Wada* in Pune, where ten families shared a single tap. Privacy did not exist. You could hear every argument, every prayer, every worry moving through thin walls.

Ours was once a respected political family. But by the time I entered the world, that legacy had dissolved. What remained was poverty — the kind that doesn't just empty your pockets, but quietly erodes dignity.

Some nights, the only thing in our kitchen was rice starch. My mother would sit beside us, smiling gently, insisting she wasn't hungry.

We knew she was.

My father worked as a farmer in our village. Most seasons barely paid. There were weeks he couldn't afford the bus fare home. He would walk miles to save a few rupees.

I remember waiting near the door, not knowing whether he would arrive that day — or the next.

His absence left silence behind.

My mother filled it.

Her strength was not loud. It did not demand recognition. It simply showed up — steady, composed, unwilling to let circumstance define our dignity. I did not understand it then. I do now.

School was not about ambition for me.

It was about survival.

Hand-me-down uniforms. Shoes worn thin. Notebooks stitched together from leftover pages of other students. While classmates carried lunchboxes and pocket money, I carried quieter questions:

Will there be dinner tonight? Will I have enough for bus fare tomorrow?

My mother would look me in the eye and say:

"Education is the only wealth no one can take from you."

That sentence shaped how I think about growth even today.

I did not study because I loved exams. I studied because I could not afford to fall behind. When electricity failed — which it often did — I studied under a kerosene lamp. When I didn't understand something, I stayed with it. Repetition became discipline. Discipline became stability.

Failure, at that stage of life, was not philosophical.

It was expensive.

Education opened doors — scholarships, admission into COEP for Mechanical Engineering, an MBA at PUMBA, and eventually a corporate career that took me across industries and countries.

From shop floors to boardrooms, from machines to strategy, the climb was steady.

From the outside, it looked complete.

The suit fit well.

And that is where the real story begins.

Somewhere in my mid-thirties, something shifted.

There was no collapse. No scandal. No dramatic failure.

Just a quiet restlessness I could not explain.

I was working longer hours than ever. Responsibility increased. My designation evolved. But the more external progress I made, the more I sensed something internally thinning.

I could navigate complex meetings without hesitation — but climbing a short flight of stairs left me breathless. I dismissed it.

I could lead teams confidently — but struggled to sit alone with my own thoughts.

Weekends — the freedom I once chased — felt strangely empty.

The uncomfortable truth was this:

I was succeeding in ways the world respected, and quietly neglecting the parts of myself that needed respect the most.

My résumé was growing.

My capacity to carry it was not.

For a long time, I refused to admit that. I told myself this was normal. That ambition required sacrifice. That fatigue was a badge of honour. That everyone at my level felt this way.

But deep down, I knew something else.

I wasn't broken.

I was misaligned.

I didn't admit that easily. I defended it longer than I'm proud of.

And misalignment is dangerous precisely because it does not look like failure.

It looks like progress.

I began asking questions I had avoided for years.

Was I truly growing — or simply accumulating experience? Was I building impact — or building endurance? Was I performing strength — or living it?

The answers were not dramatic. They were subtle. Which made them harder to ignore.

I started writing — not to publish, not to impress — but to understand the pattern I kept encountering. Every time I felt stretched or unsettled, it wasn't just workload. It was something structural.

Over time, six foundational pillars began to emerge — not as hacks, not as motivational concepts, but as supports I had either strengthened or neglected.

Physical Health.
Mindfulness.
Spiritual Grounding.
Relationships.
Financial Stability.
Growth.

When one weakened, another compensated. When one was ignored, the strain appeared somewhere else.

The realization was uncomfortable:

I had mastered complexity in business, but ignored simplicity in life.

This did not produce an overnight transformation.

It produced awareness.

I began adjusting quietly. Physical discipline I had postponed. Silence I had avoided. Conversations I had delayed. Financial clarity I had assumed would "figure itself out." Time without performance.

Nothing spectacular happened.

But something steadied.

The urgency softened. The noise reduced. Decisions felt less reactive. I was still leading, still building, still responsible for outcomes — but I was no longer operating on borrowed energy.

Opportunities continued to come. Roles expanded. Scale increased. But what changed was not the visibility of progress.

It was the stability beneath it.

Leadership began to feel less like performance and more like stewardship.

That shift is why this book exists.

This is not a how-to manual. It is not a motivational prescription. It is not a promise that alignment guarantees success.

It is an exploration of what sustains you while you pursue success.

Because the question is not whether you can build something impressive.

The question is whether you can remain whole while building it.

If you have ever felt that your effort exceeds your fulfilment… If you have sensed something is "off" despite doing everything right… If you have achieved what you once wanted and still felt restless…

You may not be failing.

You may simply be misaligned.

And misalignment, if left unexamined, compounds.

The pages ahead are reflections — experiments with awareness, adjustment, and return. Not conclusions. Not formulas. Not guarantees.

I am still learning.

But I have learned this much:

The suit can be polished. Titles can change. Recognition can rise and fall.

What endures is the condition of the life inside it.

And before we talk about success, it is worth asking —

If everything around you keeps growing, is the person inside it growing too?

Before You Read Their Stories

I started writing to understand myself.

But somewhere along the way, I kept thinking about the others.

Not characters. People.

Old friends. Colleagues. Faces from different seasons of my life. Their journeys were not identical to mine. Some had bigger titles. Some had smaller roles. Some had corner offices. Some had better coffee.

The burnout looked the same.

The exhaustion was quieter than anyone admitted. The late-night question — *"Is this really it?"* — echoed across different incomes, industries, and lifestyles.

What surprised me most was not how different we were.

It was how similar the strain felt.

When I finally stopped planning, performing, and projecting strength — and simply sat with my own thoughts — I began noticing something unsettling.

It wasn't what I had achieved.

It was what I had quietly ignored.

Sleep. Health. Stillness. Conversations I postponed. Emotions I shelved for "later." Parts of myself I assumed were strong enough to survive neglect.

They weren't.

And neither were the people around me.

There was the colleague who nodded calmly in meetings, then stayed back late to clean up what no one else wanted to handle. The friend who could light up a room but never once spoke about his father's illness. The manager who led with confidence — until the room emptied.

They were carrying something.

So was I.

Not dramatic breakdowns. Not visible crises.

Just neglected pillars — small cracks forming beneath polished surfaces.

That is how these six characters came into being.

They are not biographies. They are composites. Each one holds a fragment of something I have lived — and something I have witnessed repeatedly in others.

Arjun thought pushing harder was strength — until his body stopped agreeing.

Sana performed calm for everyone else while quietly losing it inside.

Mehul achieved everything he chased — and still felt unanchored.

Karan built independence so well that he slowly disconnected from everyone.

Pooja kept surviving each month without ever feeling secure.

Rahul mistook potential for progress and waited too long to show up.

None of them are extraordinary.

That is the point.

They are competent. Responsible. Well-meaning. Capable.

And slightly out of alignment.

For a long time, I believed exhaustion was the cost of ambition. That emotional distance was maturity. That stress was simply what leadership required.

But I began to notice a pattern.

Every time one part of life was ignored long enough, another part compensated — until it couldn't.

Health would protest.
Relationships would thin.

Meaning would fade.
Energy would fracture.

And because none of it happened overnight, it was easy to normalize.

I had mastered complexity in business.

But I had ignored simplicity in life.

By most measures, I was thriving.

Which usually meant my LinkedIn profile looked better than my blood report.

That line is not humour.

It's a warning.

There came a moment when something unsettled me more than pressure or long hours.

It was the realization that people admired the version of me that felt most disconnected inside.

The praise was landing on a performance.

And I was applauding it too.

That discomfort forced a question I had postponed for years:

Was I building a life — or maintaining an image?

The six pillars you'll encounter in these stories did not come from a seminar or a framework session. They revealed themselves in moments of strain — when I snapped at people

I cared about, ignored signals from my body, or wondered why success felt hollow.

They did not arrive dramatically.

They accumulated quietly.

These stories are not case studies. They are mirrors.

Not to expose you — but to slow you down.

You may not see yourself in all six characters.

But I would be surprised if you don't recognize something.

A sentence that feels too familiar. A reaction you've justified. A fatigue you've normalized.

If that happens, don't rush past it.

That recognition is usually where growth begins.

Most people do not pause until something forces them to.

A diagnosis.
A fractured relationship.
A moment of emotional collapse.

But misalignment does not always shout.

Sometimes it whispers.

These stories are an attempt to listen before the whisper becomes unavoidable.

They will not offer quick solutions. They will not tie themselves up neatly. They will move slowly — because real life does.

Watch how each character avoids.
Watch how they rationalize.
Watch how they return - not dramatically, but wittingly.

And as you read, ask yourself something simple:

Which part of your life feels steady — but hollow?

The cracks we ignore do not disappear.

They wait.

Arjun did not notice his — until his body made the decision for him.

That is where this book begins.

File One: Arjun's Wake-Up Call

The First File Opens

It was 2:07 AM.

The chai on my desk had gone cold. My phone buzzed with pointless WhatsApp forwards. In front of me sat a worn-out folder — **ARJUN**, scrawled in blue ink, half-faded.

"Start-up guy," I murmured.

I'd seen this story before. The late-night hustle posts. Sleep treated like weakness. Caffeine mistaken for stamina.

I opened the file.

Arjun. 32.

Once disciplined. Once steady. Now powered by urgency and Red Bull. Founder of a start-up most people nodded at without fully understanding. His life ran on calendar alerts — investor calls before breakfast, pitch decks past midnight, emails stacked over empty cans.

Chaos wasn't around him.

It had learned his name.

By 8:45 that morning — the morning everything tilted — he stood in front of a mirror adjusting his collar.

Pale face. Tired eyes.

But the smile looked expensive.

At 9:00, he was in the boardroom.
At 9:15, his slides were flawless.
At 9:32, something collapsed.

Not the pitch.

Arjun.

Flat on polished wood.

Phones dropped. Someone shouted for water. A junior whispered, "Sir… you okay?"

For once, the room that usually waited for his voice heard only silence.

That was his wake-up call.

Not applause.

Not a motivational quote.

The cold floor of a boardroom.

When he opened his eyes, there were no glass walls. No investors. Just a dull hospital ceiling and the steady beep of a monitor.

"Good morning, Mr. Superhero," the doctor said dryly. "Relax. You're not dying. Just running your body like a start-up — overworked and underfunded."

Arjun tried to laugh. It came out thin.

"What happened?"

"You fainted in front of people you were trying to impress," the doctor replied. "If you wanted attention, there are easier ways."

He flipped through the chart.

"Heart strain. Dehydration. Severe sleep debt. Stress markers through the roof. You're thirty-two going on fifty."

Thirty-two going on fifty.

The number didn't just sting.

It embarrassed him.

"I'll be fine in a few days," Arjun said automatically.

The doctor held his gaze. "You've been saying that for years."

Silence.

For the first time, Arjun didn't have a comeback.

What unsettled him wasn't the IV line in his arm.

It was the realization that his body had done what he never allowed himself to do — stop.

A nurse placed a tray beside him. Bland dal. Boiled vegetables. Food without ambition.

"Punishment?" he muttered.

"For neglect," the doctor corrected.

Sarcasm didn't land this time.

The machines, the weakness in his chest, the dryness in his throat — they left no space for performance.

A week earlier, Arjun had joked:

"Sleep is for people without Series A funding."

Now machines were regulating what ambition had ignored.

Lying there, he replayed the last five years.

Gym mornings. Measured meals. Discipline that once felt natural.

All traded for vending machine dinners and caffeine strong enough to shake his hands.

He had told himself it was temporary.

"I'll get back once this round closes."

But that sentence had quietly replaced responsibility.

Rahul — his co-founder — walked in.

"You didn't just faint," he said. "You face-planted in front of three investors."

Embarrassment flushed deeper than the IV needle.

Rahul's voice softened.

"I'm not saying stop chasing the dream. I'm saying maybe the dream doesn't require self-destruction."

Arjun stared at the ceiling.

For years, he had built resilience for pressure.

He hadn't built resilience for himself.

Discharge came quickly.

In the hospital washroom mirror, he saw someone who looked successful — and exhausted.

The founder identity still fit.

The body underneath it did not.

That night at home, he opened his fridge.

Three energy drinks. Half a pizza. Sour milk.

He stood there longer than necessary.

"I need to change," he said.

Not dramatically. Not heroically.

Just honestly.

Change didn't begin with a marathon.

It began with a glass of water.

Cold. Ordinary. Unimpressive.

He drank it slowly.

The next morning, he ate breakfast. Toast. Eggs. A banana.

It felt almost irresponsible — choosing nourishment over notifications.

He stepped outside and walked. Not for Instagram. Not for validation. Just to feel his lungs expand without panic.

The city moved fast.

For once, he didn't try to outrun it.

Work didn't soften.

Investors still called. Deadlines still pressed. The start-up still demanded.

But Arjun began making small, unfashionable decisions.

Water instead of energy drinks.

Meals instead of excuses.

Sleep before midnight — even when emails waited.

It wasn't dramatic.

No one applauded.

But something shifted.

Not his valuation.

His steadiness.

A month later, he stood in another boardroom.

Same stakes.

Same pressure.

But this time, he had slept.

He had eaten.

He wasn't vibrating on caffeine and fear.

Halfway through the pitch, he noticed something subtle.

His breathing was even.

His hands were still.

He was present.

When it ended, one investor leaned back.

"You seem calmer than last time. What changed?"

Arjun paused.

"I stopped confusing burnout for dedication."

No humour.

No performance.

Just truth.

That night, he wrote in his notebook:

Discipline isn't about extracting productivity from every hour. It's about protecting the body that carries you through those hours.

He underlined it once.

He had chased abs once.

Then headlines.

Now he was chasing sustainability.

He hadn't transformed overnight.

He still slipped. Still overworked. Still relapsed into old habits.

But now he noticed sooner.

And noticing shortened the damage.

Health hadn't collapsed in one day.

It had frayed quietly.

And it began to rebuild the same way.

Quietly.

File #1 closed.

Arjun didn't conquer balance.

He simply stopped ignoring the cost of pretending he didn't need it.

And that changed the direction of everything that followed.

File Two: Sana and the CEO Breakdown

The Second File Opens

12:41 a.m.

The street outside was silent. My room wasn't. Open files, coffee stains, a flickering laptop screen. And in the corner, a blue-tagged folder I'd avoided all night.

SANA.

"Marketing prodigy," I muttered. "Always on. Always perfect."

I opened the file.

Sana, twenty-five. The kind of employee start-ups brag about. Sharp, articulate, the unofficial "pitch whisperer." Her Instagram looked curated — matcha mornings, yoga mats, balanced living. But if you watched closely, you could see it. The slight blur in her stories where exhaustion tried to slip through.

Her days began before sunrise. "New York clients," she'd say, headset already on. Her calendar was a grid of color-coded control. If it wasn't scheduled, it didn't exist.

It used to be a joke.

It wasn't anymore.

The breakdown didn't arrive dramatically.

It happened mid-sentence.

6:58 p.m. Zoom call. Camera on. Posture straight. Voice calm.

Slide one — sharp insight.
Slide two — bold strategy.
Slide three —

Her throat tightened.

The cursor blinked on the screen. Waiting.

"Sana?" the CEO asked. "Are you there?"

She tried to answer. Nothing came.

Her hands trembled. Her screen froze. Her eyes didn't.

The first tear surprised her.

She reached for mute and hit "Leave Meeting" instead.

Silence.

Just her reflection in a black screen.

Mascara smudged. Shoulders stiff. Breath shallow.

"What was that?" she whispered.

Her phone buzzed.

"Take two days off," her manager texted. "Mental wellness break."

The emoji at the end felt unnecessary.

Two days.

Her mind had been fraying for months.

I paused there.

Most breakdowns don't look dramatic. They look like freezing mid-sentence. The body still, the mind in flames.

I kept reading.

The next morning, she didn't open her laptop.

148 unread emails.

She didn't touch them.

Instead, she called her mother.

The moment she heard her voice, something cracked again — not panic this time, just release. Tears without explanation.

"Beta," her mother said softly, "breathe."

One word.

It landed harder than every productivity podcast she had half-listened to.

She realized she hadn't taken a full breath in months.

That evening, she sat across from a therapist for the first time.

She had almost cancelled twice.

"I don't know what's wrong," she said.

The therapist nodded. "How long have you been pretending to be fine?"

Sana stared at the tissue box between them.

"I don't know."

"That's where most people start."

Silence followed.

It felt uncomfortable.

And necessary.

The first night she tried sitting in quiet, she lasted three minutes.

Her mind rebelled.

Deadlines. Messages. Embarrassing memories from years ago. What-ifs stacked over what-next.

"This is pointless," she muttered.

But she stayed.

The next day, she deleted Instagram.

Her thumb hovered longer than she expected. It wasn't addiction — it was attachment. The illusion of relevance. The reassurance that she was visible.

When the app disappeared, so did the noise.

At first, the silence felt loud.

Then it felt honest.

Work did not slow down.

Deadlines still pressed. Clients still demanded. Slack still pinged.

But Sana began making smaller, quieter changes.

She stopped answering messages after midnight.

The first time she did it, anxiety followed her into bed.

The second time, sleep did.

A week later, her boss asked her to lead another major pitch.

Her pulse quickened.

The old reflex was immediate — say yes, over prepare, outperform.

Instead, she paused.

"I'll join," she said slowly. "But I won't lead this one."

There was a brief silence on the call.

"Alright," her boss replied. "That works."

It was a small sentence.

It felt like reclaiming oxygen.

When she returned to the office after her break, nothing had changed.

Same glass doors. Same emails. Same urgency.

Only she felt different.

A junior rushed to her desk. "Can you take this campaign too?"

The answer rose automatically — yes.

She stopped it.

"I can't right now."

The words surprised even her.

They weren't defensive.

They were steady.

Weeks later, the real test came.

A client shifted their brief hours before a deadline. The team spiralled.

Voices overlapped. Panic climbed the room.

Old Sana would have absorbed it all. Fixed everything. Stayed late. Collapsed quietly later.

This time, she said, "Let's pause for five minutes."

Someone groaned. "We don't have time."

"Then we need it," she replied.

They paused.

Just five minutes.

When they resumed, the room felt different. Not calm — just clearer.

The work got done.

Not perfectly.

But without anyone breaking mid-sentence.

That night, she wrote one line in her notebook:

I'm not trying to eliminate chaos. I'm learning not to collapse inside it.

She closed the journal without underlining it.

It didn't feel profound.

It felt accurate.

The anxiety didn't disappear.

Some mornings it returned — shallow breath, tight chest, racing thoughts.

The difference now was smaller than she expected.

She noticed sooner.

She breathed before reacting.

She let the thoughts speak without obeying them.

Presence didn't feel dramatic.

It felt uneventful.

And steady.

Months later, someone asked her, "How do you stay calm during chaos?"

She considered the question.

"I don't," she said. "I just stopped feeding it."

They laughed.

She didn't.

Because she knew how close she had come to mistaking noise for importance.

Mindfulness hadn't made her slower.

It had made her aware.

Aware of when she was spiralling.
Aware of when she was performing.
Aware of when silence felt unbearable.

And slowly, silence stopped feeling like an enemy.

File #2 closed.

Sana didn't conquer her mind.

She simply stopped running from it.

And in that pause, she found something she had been chasing for years without knowing it.

Space.

File Three: Mehul's Inner Reboot

The Third File Opens

The applause lasted longer than it should have.

Lights flashed. Cameras caught his angle. Someone handed him a trophy heavy enough to feel important.

Mehul smiled.

It was the correct smile. Measured. Confident. Grateful.

When he stepped off stage, the noise followed him — congratulations, shoulder claps, a dozen phones pointed in his direction.

Later that night, alone in his apartment, the trophy sat on the table.

It reflected light perfectly.

It reflected nothing else.

He stood there longer than necessary.

"You got what you wanted," he muttered.

The room did not argue.

For years, he had chased markers — promotions, valuation jumps, awards, titles that sounded like altitude.

Each time he reached one, he raised the bar before he could feel it.

That night, for the first time, he didn't raise it.

And the silence underneath startled him.

It wasn't sadness.

It wasn't even disappointment.

It was absence.

He had built momentum.

He wasn't sure he had built meaning.

Two days later, the meeting cracked.

Vikram cut him off mid-sentence.

"Maybe if you actually listened—"

"You always do this," Mehul snapped.

The room froze.

It wasn't about strategy anymore. It hadn't been for months.

It was about control.

About being right.

About proving superiority in rooms that didn't require it.

Vikram pushed back his chair and walked out.

The door shut harder than necessary.

For a moment, Mehul felt the familiar surge — justification, anger, certainty.

Then something else.

Fear.

Not of losing the argument.

Of recognizing himself in it.

Later, when a junior stumbled through a presentation, Mehul opened his mouth to interrupt.

He didn't.

He let the silence stretch.

It felt unnatural.

It also felt strong.

That night, he couldn't sleep.

The trophy still sat on the table.

He turned it away from him.

For the first time in years, he asked a question he had avoided:

When did I stop liking the man I became?

The answer did not arrive.

But the question stayed.

A week later, there was a leadership offsite.

Green lawns. Glass conference rooms. "Reset" printed on banners.

It felt staged.

During dinner, laughter echoed too loudly.

Mehul stepped away.

He walked toward the artificial lake behind the property.

The surface was still.

He crouched and looked at his reflection.

No title hovered above it.

No applause followed it.

Just a tired man staring back.

He did nothing.

He didn't try to solve anything.

He didn't search for insight.

He just stayed there.

The stillness did not feel profound.

It felt unfamiliar.

The next morning, while others prepared slides, Mehul sat outside with tea.

No phone.

No notebook.

Just ten quiet minutes.

His thoughts were not kind.

They ran fast. Accusatory.

You've built everything on noise. You don't know who you are without urgency. If you slow down, you'll disappear.

He almost stood up.

Instead, he stayed.

Nothing changed. Except that he didn't run.

Back in the city, work resumed at full speed.

Deadlines didn't soften.

People didn't become easier.

But Mehul began experimenting with one small act:

Pause before reply.

It felt inefficient. It also felt honest.

When Vikram eventually asked, "Coffee?" Mehul said yes.

They didn't solve the company.

They didn't rewrite strategy.

They spoke without defending.

When they left, nothing had been fixed.

Something had been released.

A few days later, Mehul visited his parents.

No announcements. No dramatic confession.

Just dinner at the same wooden table.

After the plates were cleared, his father said quietly, “You look tired.”

“Not from work,” Mehul replied. “From… noise.”

His father nodded.

“Peace isn’t something you reach,” he said. “It’s something you stop running from.”

There was no lecture.

No philosophy.

Just tea between them.

That night, Mehul slept without scrolling.

Back home, he began waking ten minutes earlier.

He did not meditate.

He did not chant.

He simply sat.

Some mornings were restless.

Some were dull.

Some were heavy.

But gradually, the urgency lost volume.

Not gone.

Just softer.

He noticed something else.

Ambition didn't disappear when silence arrived.

It clarified.

In meetings, he stopped competing for the last word.

When a team member made a mistake, he responded slower.

Not to appear calm.

To remain aligned.

Someone once told him, "You've changed."

He answered without thinking, "I just stopped auditioning for peace."

Months later, another award ceremony arrived.

Same lights.

Same applause.

He accepted the trophy.

This time, he felt neither rush nor emptiness.

Just a moment.

Finite.

Contained.

When he returned home, he placed it on the shelf.

He did not stare at it.

He did not question it.

He turned off the lights.

Sat on the balcony.

The city buzzed below.

His phone vibrated beside him.

He didn't pick it up.

Not out of discipline.

Out of choice.

The silence no longer accused him.

It held him.

He exhaled.

For the first time in years, he wasn't trying to become someone.

He was simply present with who he already was.

File #3 closed.

Mehul didn’t find spirituality.

He stopped outsourcing his identity to applause.

And in that stillness, ambition finally had something solid to stand on.

File Four: Karan's Lone Wolf Syndrome

The Fourth File Opens

The email arrived at 9:18 p.m.

Subject: Leadership Announcement.

Karan clicked it before it fully loaded.

He had already pictured the line.
He had already rehearsed the modest smile.

It wasn't his name.

It was Arnav's.

Karan didn't swear. He didn't slam the desk. He just read the sentence twice, as if a second reading might correct it.

It didn't.

The office was loud the next morning. Cake. Photos. Laughter near Arnav's desk.

Karan stood by the printer, pretending to fix a paper jam that wasn't there.

No one asked how he was.

By afternoon, Rajat called him in.

"You're exceptional at execution," Rajat said. "But leadership isn't only execution."

Karan leaned back. "Let me guess. I need to 'connect.'"

Rajat didn't smile. "You deliver. But people don't feel seen by you."

"That's not my job," Karan replied.

Rajat held his gaze. "That's exactly the job."

The sentence stayed longer than the promotion loss.

That night, Karan microwaved dinner and sat at the table with his phone face-up.

He scrolled through his contacts.

Gym. Clients. Vendors. Numbers.

No one he could call without a reason.

Three missed calls from Amma blinked at the top.

He didn't press dial.

He turned the phone over.

The silence felt earned.

The cross-team project began two days later.

Twelve people. Three departments. Too many opinions.

Within twenty minutes, Karan had reorganized the entire plan in his head.

Within thirty, he was explaining it out loud.

By forty, the room had stopped contributing.

After the meeting, Mira — the intern — caught him near the elevator.

“Sir, can I say something?”

“Go on.”

“You don’t leave space,” she said. “People stop thinking when you start fixing.”

He almost dismissed it.

He didn’t.

“What did I miss?” he asked.

“Ravi had a vendor lead. Shreya had drafted outreach. You cut both.”

He walked back to his desk slower than usual.

At the next meeting, he tried something unnatural.

"I spoke too much yesterday," he said. "Let's start with updates."

The silence was uncomfortable.

Then Ravi spoke.

Then Shreya.

The ideas weren't perfect.

They were workable.

He felt the urge to correct.

He didn't.

When the meeting ended, Mira gave a small nod.

Not approval.

Just acknowledgment.

It was enough.

That evening, he finally called his mother.

"Busy?" she asked gently.

"Not today," he said.

She didn't interrogate. She just talked about dinner plans and the neighbour's new dog.

He listened.

When the call ended, nothing dramatic had changed. But the room felt less sharp.

Midweek brought a client escalation.

The old reflex returned instantly — take over, fix everything, control the chaos.

Instead, he gathered the team.

"Two tracks," he said. "Ravi on the patch. Shreya on client communication. Mira track blockers. I'll stay on the call."

The bug was fixed by evening.

The client calmed.

The team logged off before midnight.

No one applauded.

They just said, "Good work."

It felt… shared.

Days passed.

Some meetings went well.

Some didn't.

He still interrupted sometimes.

He noticed it faster.

Once, Shreya stopped mid-sentence and looked at him.

He caught himself.

"Sorry. Continue."

Small correction.

Big shift.

A week later, Rajat stopped by his desk.

"Different energy lately," he said.

"I'm trying not to solve everything," Karan replied.

Rajat nodded. "Trust takes longer than talent."

That night, instead of staying late alone, Karan bought four cups of chai on his way back from a call.

He placed them on the table without a speech.

"Break," he said.

Ravi blinked. "From you?"

"Don't get used to it."

They laughed.

It wasn't bonding.

It wasn't team-building.

It was ten minutes without hierarchy.

He realized he hadn't laughed at work in months.

Promotion talk didn't return immediately.

No second email.

No dramatic reversal.

Just work.

One afternoon, Ravi sent a team-wide update about a small win and copied everyone.

Karan's name wasn't mentioned.

He read it.

Closed the mail.

And felt lighter than he expected.

On Sunday, he met an old college friend for badminton.

He was out of breath in five minutes.

They sat afterward with cutting chai, sweat drying in the sun.

“You’re quieter,” his friend said.

“Maybe,” Karan replied.

“Used to feel like you were competing with the room.”

He thought about that.

“Maybe I was.”

The silence between them was easy.

He didn’t check his phone.

Back at work, the cross-team project slowly found rhythm.

Not because Karan led it.

Because the team owned it.

In a meeting, Mira disagreed with him directly.

He listened.

She was right.

He said so.

The room didn't freeze.

It continued.

That was new.

One evening, he stayed back alone again.

Not out of isolation.

Just to think.

He opened his notebook — the old one filled with "Be faster" and "Don't depend on anyone."

He tore out a page.

Wrote a new line:

Efficiency built my career. People will decide how far it goes.

He closed it.

Turned off the lights.

Walked out without headphones.

The city noise felt less like competition.

More like company.

The next morning, he reached the office early and made tea.

Not as strategy.
Not as redemption.
Just because it felt normal.

Mira walked in.

"Early morning chai club?" she asked.

"Only for people who show up," he said.

She took a cup and stood beside him. Steam rose between them. The office lights were still warming up. No one else had arrived.

For a few minutes, neither of them spoke.

It wasn't awkward.

It wasn't profound.

It was ordinary.

Later that day, during a review, he interrupted Ravi again.

Halfway through the sentence, he caught himself.

"Sorry," he said. "Go on."

Ravi continued.

No one reacted. No one praised the correction.

The meeting moved forward.

That evening, as the office emptied, Karan stayed back for a moment.

Not because he needed to fix anything.

Just to notice the room.

A month ago, he had filled every silence.

Now, some of them held.

His phone buzzed — Amma calling.

He answered.

“Reached home?” she asked.

“Leaving now,” he said.

“Eat properly,” she added.

“I will,” he replied.

He meant it.

He turned off the lights, picked up his bag, and stepped into the corridor.

The city outside was loud as always.

For once, he didn’t feel like he had to outpace it.

He walked toward the elevator — not alone, not leading, not proving.

Just part of the building he used to treat like a battlefield.

File #4 closed.

Karan didn't transform into a different man. He simply learned to stay in the room — even when he wasn't the loudest voice in it.

And that was enough to begin.

File Five: Pooja and the Art of Not Drowning

The Fifth File Opens

The folder says **POOJA**.

The last letter is smudged.

Twenty-nine.
Single mother.
Three jobs.

One son who still believes parathas are magic.

On paper, she looks resilient. In real life, she is a ledger with a heartbeat.

Her mornings begin before the city decides to exist.

Uniform ironed.
Tiffin packed.

Water bottle filled.
Gas turned off twice.

By 6:15, she is already calculating.

Not dreams.

Numbers.

Rent.
School fee.
Electricity.
Transport.
Loan.

Every rupee has an assignment. Nothing floats freely.

She doesn't complain. Complaining wastes time.

The recovery agent arrives on a Tuesday.

She is holding a ribbon for her son's school performance when the doorbell rings.

The man wears a suit that looks too sharp for her small living room.

"Payment pending," he says.

Her son walks in wearing a paper crown.

"Amma, look."

For a second, she considers not opening the door fully. For a second, she wishes the room would shrink.

The man flips through papers as if they are more real than the child.

Humiliation is quiet. It doesn't shout.

It stands in your house and asks for signatures.

She negotiates. Promises dates she is not sure she can keep. Signs what she must.

He leaves.

The ribbon remains on the counter.

That night she lies awake.

Not because of the amount.

Because her son saw the interruption.

The next morning, she opens her notebook.

For the first time, she writes every expense.

Exact numbers.
No rounding.
No guessing.

The list is longer than she expected.

She feels the familiar urge to stop midway.

She doesn't.

When the page ends, she turns it and continues.

The problem shrinks slightly once it has edges.

She cuts small things first.

Subscription cancelled.
Outside tea stopped.
Auto ride replaced with bus twice a week.

The savings are unimpressive.

But they are visible. Visibility matters.

The agent returns three days later.

This time she does not pretend surprise.

"You can come only on Fridays," she says. "Ten to eleven."

He blinks. "Madam—"

"Friday," she repeats.

It is not aggression. It is structure.

He agrees.

After he leaves, her son asks, "Is he angry?"

"He's doing his job," she replies. "And I'm doing mine."

The sentence steadies her more than him.

Work remains heavy.

Emails pile up.
Requests expand.
Colleagues assume availability.

Earlier, she would have absorbed everything.

Now she asks, "Is it urgent?"

If the answer is no, it waits.

If it is yes, she handles it.

No extra apology.

At 6:55 p.m., she closes her system.

"I won't be available after seven," she tells her manager.

He studies her face.

"Okay," he says.

The world does not collapse.

Friday, 10:03 a.m.

The agent arrives.

She seats him at the dining table.

"What is the minimum for now?" she asks.

He tells her.

She writes it down.

"I can pay in ten days. Not earlier."

He adjusts his file.

"Ten days."

"Only Fridays," she adds.

He nods.

No raised voices.

No pleading.

When he leaves, she sits still for a moment.

Not victorious.

Just less exposed.

That evening, she spreads all papers on the table.

Bills.
Receipts.
Loan statements.

Her son draws beside her.

"Red or blue?" he asks.

"Blue," she replies.

"You didn't even see."

"You always choose blue."

He laughs.

She continues sorting.

One pile for essentials.
One for debt.
One for unnecessary leakage.

It is messy.

It is honest.

For the first time, the papers do not feel like accusations.

They feel like tasks.

She calls her mother.

"I need help," she says.

There is no lecture on the other side.

“Come Sunday,” her mother replies. “Bring everything.”

The word everything feels heavy.

And relieving.

At the bank, she negotiates.

“I need a revised schedule.”

The clerk glances at her file.

“You must stick to it.”

“I will.”

She signs new terms.

Walking out, she does not feel rich.

She feels structured.

The next recovery visit is calm.

He comes at ten.

She pays the partial amount.

They schedule the next date.

No neighbour watches this time.

No paper crown in the background.

Just paperwork.

Paperwork is manageable.

Her son's school performance arrives.

The same ribbon rests on his shoulder.

She sits in the second row.

He searches for her face before speaking.

When he finds it, his shoulders relax.

He finishes without stumbling.

Afterward, the teacher says, "He's confident when you're here."

She nods.

Confidence, she realizes, is also built from routine.

At work, a junior approaches her.

"How do you plan expenses?" he asks.

She opens her notebook.

"Divide into three," she says. "Must pay. Can delay. Don't need."

He listens carefully.

"And it works?"

"It works if you follow it."

She closes the notebook.

She did not expect to teach this.

Weeks pass.

There are still bills.

Still pressure.

Still late evenings.

But the panic is different.

It does not flood the room.

It knocks.

She decides when to open the door.

One night, she finds her son asleep with his homework open.

She moves the notebook aside and lifts him gently.

His hand grips her shirt even in sleep.

She stands there longer than necessary.

The ribbon from that first Tuesday lies folded neatly inside his school bag.

Not forgotten.

Just placed properly.

Sunday afternoon.

Tea on the balcony.

No calls.

No unexpected knocks.

Her notebook lies open beside her.

The numbers have not disappeared.

But they are aligned.

Her son climbs onto her lap.

“Mama, are we okay now?”

She looks at the page.

Then at him.

“We’re handling it,” she says.

He nods, satisfied.

She closes the notebook.

For the first time in years, she is not trying to swim faster than the current.

She is learning where the current bends.

File #5 closed.

Pooja did not become wealthy.

She became deliberate.

And deliberate people rarely drown.

File Six: Rahul and the Myth of Talent

The Sixth File Opens

The folder says **RAHUL**.

Twenty-six.
Brilliant on paper.
Unreliable in motion.

A degree with distinction. Two hackathon trophies. One framed newspaper clipping his mother still keeps in plastic.

And twenty-two unfinished applications.

Rahul always said he was waiting for "the right moment."

The moment never arrived.

His room looked like deferred ambition.

Half-read books.
Three browser tabs titled *New Plan*.
A whiteboard that still said *Goals 2023*.

It was 12:48 p.m.

His interview was at 1:00.

"Rahul! Your interview!" his cousin called from the hallway.

"I know," he replied, not moving.

He stared at the ceiling as if motivation might fall from it.

The meeting link expired at 1:07.

He watched it disappear.

Meera called at 3:12.

"Did you attend?" she asked.

He hesitated.

"Rahul… are you even interested in this job?"

"I am."

"Then why don't you show up?"

He had no answer that didn't sound like an excuse.

She wasn't angry anymore. That would have been easier.

“I can’t keep pushing you,” she said quietly. “You think about trying. That’s not the same as trying.”

The call ended without drama.

The room felt heavier.

He opened his inbox.

Fourteen rejections.
Eleven unfinished courses.
Three half-written cover letters that all began with confidence and ended with silence.

He wasn’t stupid.

He was inconsistent.

There is a difference.

Varun came over the next afternoon.

“You’re not lazy,” Varun said, scanning the room. “You’re undisciplined.”

“That’s the same thing.”

“No,” Varun replied calmly. “Lazy people don’t care. You care. You just don’t finish.”

The sentence stayed.

"You waste talent," Varun added. "And that's worse."

Rahul didn't argue.

He set an alarm for 9 a.m.

It rang.

He turned it off.

Woke at 12:42.

Stared at the ceiling.

"Can't even wake up," he muttered.

The shame this time wasn't defensive.

It was precise.

That afternoon he cleaned his desk.

Not the whole room.

Just the desk.

He threw away empty packets. Stacked papers. Closed irrelevant tabs.

Under a pile of books, he found an old notebook.

Three years ago, he had written:

Do one thing every day. Just one.

He closed it slowly.

The next morning, he woke at 10:15.

Not victory.

But movement.

He opened a coding site.

The first problem took him ten minutes to read.

He solved half of it.

Instead of quitting, he stayed.

Thirty-five minutes total.

He logged off.

It counted.

He wrote three instructions and taped them above his desk:

Wake before 10.
Finish one task.
Step outside once.

No quotes.

No inspiration.

Just instructions.

A week passed.

He didn't transform.

He woke between 9:30 and 10:10. Finished small tasks. Submitted one full application without deleting it five times.

The room began to look less like a waiting area.

Then came the interview.

Online.

Midway through, the recruiter asked:

"There's a gap this year. What happened?"

He could have blamed the market.
Burnout.
Family issues.

He didn't.

"I stopped showing up," he said. "I'm fixing that."

The recruiter nodded and moved on.

No judgment.

No rescue.

Just acknowledgment.

Rahul logged off feeling lighter.

He had told the truth without defending himself.

He didn't get that job.

He folded his clothes that evening anyway.

Finished another coding problem.

Called his mother before she called him.

"I'm working on things," he said.

She didn't ask for proof.

"I know," she replied.

This time he believed her.

Three days later, a start-up founder messaged.

"Still open to freelancing?"

It wasn't glamorous.

It was work.

He replied immediately.

"Yes."

When the brief arrived, he didn't rush.

He read it twice.
Made notes.
Asked one clarifying question instead of pretending.

He delivered on time.

The founder called.

"This is solid. Want to continue?"

Rahul paused.

"Yes."

Not excited.

Ready.

Work didn't fix everything.

Some mornings he still reached for his phone before brushing his teeth.

Sometimes he stared at a task longer than necessary.

But he didn't disappear anymore.

When another rejection email came, he read it.

Closed it. Opened the next file.

That was new.

Weeks later, he ran into Meera outside a grocery store.

"You look different," she said.

"I'm consistent," he replied.

She smiled faintly.

"That's new."

There was no reunion.

No promise.

Just recognition.

One evening, his neighbour's son knocked.

"Can you help me with this loop?"

Rahul leaned over the notebook.

He didn't over explain.

He didn't perform intelligence.

He showed him how to break the problem down.

After the boy left, Rahul sat quietly.

Teaching required patience.

Patience required staying.

The start-up expanded his role.

More responsibility.

More deadlines.

He felt the old instinct — overcommit, then collapse.

Instead, he wrote three tasks for the day.

Finished two.

Carried one forward without guilt.

The rhythm mattered more than speed.

One morning he woke before his alarm.

No surge of motivation.
No dramatic clarity.
Just readiness.

He looked at his desk.

Clean.
Not perfect.
Usable.

He opened his notebook and wrote:

Show up today.

Nothing else.

He didn't underline it.
He didn't decorate it.

He began.

He still had talent.

That had never been the issue.

What changed was smaller.

He stopped negotiating with tomorrow.

He worked. Uncertain. Still working.

File #6 closed.

Rahul was never a lazy genius. He was a disciplined beginner who finally believed himself.

And belief, practiced daily, is just another form of work.

The Quiet Balance

I did not expect these stories to teach me anything new.

They came from my own life. I believed I had already understood them. Experience, I assumed, automatically matured into wisdom.

It doesn't.

Something changed while writing them.

When you turn memories into characters, they stop obeying you. They speak with clarity you avoided when you were busy surviving them. They show you not just what happened — but who you were while it was happening.

For years, I kept moving without asking why certain parts of my life felt uneven. I assumed imbalance was the natural tax for ambition.

If you wanted something badly enough, you carried the weight.
If it grew heavier, you adjusted your grip.

That was my rule.

But as these six lives unfolded on paper, I began to see something I had missed while living through them.

They were not separate problems.

They were connected signals.

Arjun was the season when I confused stamina with strength. Sleep became negotiable. Rest felt indulgent. I treated my body as background infrastructure — reliable, silent, compliant. I forgot that it keeps score.

Sana was the version of me who functioned impressively while feeling internally distant. I answered every external demand but avoided internal questions. I mistook emotional suppression for discipline.

Mehul reflected a quieter phase — when achievement continued, but meaning thinned. Nothing was wrong. Yet nothing felt anchored. It wasn't crisis. It was absence.

Karan revealed how easily relationships fade when attention is replaced with assumption. Disconnection rarely arrives loudly. It grows in small postponements.

Pooja exposed something I resisted admitting — financial stress reshapes your posture toward life long before it changes your lifestyle. Movement without clarity creates fragile stability.

And Rahul reminded me that growth does not respond to brilliance. It responds to consistency. I had mistaken motion for direction more often than I realized.

As I stepped back, the pattern became obvious.

Life does not fracture in isolated corners.

It shifts systemically.

When physical health weakens, patience shortens. When emotional steadiness erodes, relationships absorb tension.

When financial uncertainty grows, fear influences decisions. When identity is tied too tightly to achievement, growth becomes anxious.

Nothing operates alone.

I did not set out to build a model.

I was trying to understand why some seasons felt grounded while others felt unstable despite visible success.

What emerged was not a theory — but a structure I began to notice.

Life seemed to rest on a handful of interdependent supports.

Physical health — the base that quietly carries everything else. Without energy, judgment strains. With recovery, clarity sharpens.

Mindfulness — the ability to pause before reacting. Without awareness, urgency disguises itself as importance.

Spiritual grounding — not ritual, but orientation. When worth depends solely on performance, every setback becomes a threat. Grounding steadies' identity beyond metrics.

Relationships — the mirrors that keep success from becoming isolating. They remind you who you are outside of what you produce.

Financial stability — not excess, but sufficiency. Enough to reduce the quiet fear that leaks into decision-making.

And growth — the forward motion that keeps life evolving. But growth without grounding becomes restless expansion.

For years, I thought imbalance meant poor time management.

Now I understand it differently.

Imbalance often means one area is absorbing more strain than it was designed to hold.

Balance is not equal distribution.

It is responsiveness.

It is noticing which part is asking for care — and tending to it before neglect spreads into the rest.

This realization did not make life simpler.

It made it honest.

It changed the questions I ask myself.

Am I tired because I am ambitious — or because I am not recovering? Am I restless because I need growth — or because I lack grounding? Am I anxious about work — or about security? Am I independent — or disconnected?

Clarity begins with better questions.

The Quiet Balance is not about controlling every area of life.

It is about remaining aware of them.

We rarely collapse dramatically.

We drift.

One late night becomes a pattern.
One postponed conversation becomes distance.
One ignored signal becomes fatigue.
One compromise becomes habit.

The drift is subtle.

So is the correction.

You do not need a dramatic reinvention.

You need attention.

Attention to what feels strained.
Attention to what feels neglected.
Attention to what you keep postponing.

If you recognized yourself in fragments throughout this book, that recognition is not accidental.

It is the beginning of responsibility.

Not responsibility to become flawless.

Responsibility to remain engaged.

You will still overwork.
You will still overthink.
You will still misjudge seasons.

I do.

The difference is noticing sooner.

The difference is adjusting earlier.

This book does not end with answers.

It ends with awareness.

Awareness is not passive.

It is direction.

You don't need a dramatic overhaul.

You need to stop neglecting what already knows it needs attention.

In the end, the world may remember what you built.

But you will live with the condition in which you built it.

The body that carried you.
The mind that processed the pressure.

The relationships that stood beside you.
The quiet moments you either ignored or honoured.

The ones where the house is finally silent, and you realize you don't know what to do without noise.

Success is not the summit you reach.

It is the way you stand while climbing.

And long after the climb is forgotten, you will still be living in the structure you built within yourself.

Build that evenly.

Not loudly.

Just steadily enough that you can remain inside it —

without needing to escape it.

That is the balance.

Letters to My Younger Self

There are things I understand now that I did not understand then.

Not because I lacked intelligence. Because I lacked distance.

If I could sit across from the younger version of myself — ambitious, impatient, convinced that speed was strength — I would not try to slow him down.

I would try to sharpen his awareness.

This is not regret. It is perspective earned through misalignment.

You Are Not Behind

There were seasons when I measured myself against people I barely knew. Their promotions. Their funding rounds. Their timelines.

I assumed momentum meant maturity.

It doesn't.

Growth that arrives before internal stability often creates pressure that discipline alone cannot sustain.

Speed impresses.
Stability endures.

It took me longer than necessary to understand that.

Exhaustion Is Not Discipline

There was a period when fatigue felt like proof. Long hours signalled commitment. Rest felt negotiable.

What I did not recognize was how exhaustion quietly alters judgment.
Patience shortens.
Clarity narrows.
Reactivity increases.

The body does not argue loudly. It accumulates.

By the time it speaks clearly, the cost is higher than the effort that caused it.

Energy, not image, determines sustainability.

Pause Before Reaction

Earlier in my career, speed of response felt like competence.

Often it was insecurity.

Not every disagreement required correction. Not every silence required filling.

The capacity to pause is less about restraint and more about control.

Measured response builds credibility faster than quick defence.

Role Is Temporary. Identity Is Not.

There were years when my title carried more weight than my internal stability.

That imbalance is subtle.

When worth attaches itself to performance, every setback feels personal.

Roles evolve.
Markets shift.
Recognition fluctuates.

Identity must be anchored somewhere deeper than designation.

It took time to separate what I do from who I am.

That separation created steadiness.

Relationships Fade Quietly

I did not lose people dramatically.

Distance grew through postponement. Through distracted conversations. Through assuming there would be time later.

There is rarely “later.”

Attention is not a courtesy.
It is structure.

Neglect does not explode.
It erodes.

By the time absence is visible, the gap has already widened.

Financial Literacy Is Emotional Stability

For many years, I focused on income.

I did not focus enough on understanding money.

Revenue is not security. Cash flow is not clarity. Growth is not stability.

Financial illiteracy creates background anxiety — subtle, constant, unspoken. It influences decisions long before numbers demand it.

When I began understanding how money moves — liquidity, risk exposure, leverage, long-term structure — my posture toward opportunity changed.

Calmer decisions followed.

Financial literacy is not about accumulation. It is about reducing uncertainty.

The more clearly you understand your financial architecture, the less reactive your ambition becomes.

That understanding should not be outsourced entirely. It shapes more than balance sheets. It shapes behaviour.

Growth Is Direction, Not Expansion

There were seasons when expansion felt like proof of progress.

Adding roles. Adding commitments. Adding scale.

What I learned later is that expansion without stabilization creates fragility.

Direction matters more than volume.

Consistency compounds quietly. Ambition alone does not.

The Need to Prove

Much of my early drive was fuelled by proving.

Belonging had to be earned. Capability had to be demonstrated repeatedly.

Eventually, I realized the evaluation was largely internal.

The pressure was self-constructed.

Work built from insecurity feels different from work built from steadiness.

The output may look identical.

The internal cost is not.

Silence Is Structural

Stillness once felt inefficient.

Silence felt uncomfortable.

In quiet moments, unresolved questions surface.

Avoiding them does not dissolve them. It delays them.

When I began sitting with uncertainty instead of distracting myself from it, clarity improved.

Not instantly.
But progressively.

Silence is not emptiness.
It is diagnostic.

Balance Is Ongoing Correction

I once assumed balance was a destination.

It is not.

Life expands.
Responsibilities multiply.
Energy fluctuates.

Balance is responsiveness.

When strain appears, adjust.
When neglect surfaces, restore.

Earlier correction prevents larger repair.

That is maturity.

If there is one principle that integrates all of this, it is simple:

Do not build a life that appears strong but rests on unstable foundations.

Strength is not measured by how much you can carry.

It is measured by how early you recognize misalignment.

I still misjudge seasons.
I still overextend.
I still recalibrate.

The difference now is awareness.

Awareness shortens damage.
Awareness stabilizes growth.
Awareness changes the quality of what is built — and the condition of the person building it.

That is what distance has taught me.

And that is what I would offer my younger self — not instruction, but clarity.

Principles of Quiet Balance

Endurance without recovery degrades performance.

Velocity without structural stability increases fragility.

Expansion without grounding amplifies internal volatility.

Revenue without financial clarity sustains hidden risk.

Ambition without operating discipline compounds strain.

Talent without reliability erodes credibility.

Unexamined silence accumulates unresolved pressure.

Deferred conversations normalize distance.

Delayed correction multiplies consequence.

Applied awareness reduces preventable damage.

Before You Close This Book

If you have reached this page, something in these stories likely stayed with you.

Maybe it was Arjun's collapse.
Or Sana's pause.
Or Mehul's silence.
Or Karan's correction.
Or Pooja's structure.
Or Rahul's small consistency.

Or maybe it was none of them — and it was you.

This book was never meant to give you answers.

It was meant to make you notice.

But noticing is not passive.

It carries responsibility.

Not responsibility to transform overnight.
Not responsibility to fix everything at once.
Just responsibility to remain aware.

If you are reading this as an individual, the work is quiet.

Sleep when you need to.
Pause before reacting.
Have the conversation you keep postponing.
Look at the numbers you avoid.
Finish what you start.
Adjust before strain becomes collapse.

That is enough.

But if you are reading this as a leader, the responsibility expands.

Your imbalance does not stay private.

It becomes culture.

If you normalize overwork, your team will hide exhaustion.
If you avoid difficult conversations, silence becomes policy.
If you chase growth without grounding, urgency becomes identity.
If you ignore financial clarity, anxiety becomes strategy.

Organizations rarely fracture suddenly.

They drift.

One rushed decision.
One ignored tension.
One postponed realignment.
One leader too tired to notice.

Systems absorb the strain until they cannot.

The same way individuals do.

The six pillars do not apply only to people. They apply to enterprises.

Physical health becomes operational capacity.
Mindfulness becomes strategic pause.
Spiritual grounding becomes purpose beyond quarterly metrics.
Relationships become trust capital.
Financial stability becomes optionality.
Growth becomes disciplined expansion.

When one weakens, another compensates.

For a while.

If you build aggressively but recover poorly, culture erodes.
If you optimize numbers but neglect trust, momentum thins.
If you pursue valuation but abandon clarity, direction blurs.

Leadership is not about controlling every pillar.

It is about sensing which one is under strain.

And responding before the strain spreads.

You do not need dramatic restructuring.

You need attention.

Attention to fatigue — in yourself and in your team.
Attention to conversations avoided.
Attention to where fear is shaping decisions.
Attention to whether growth feels aligned — or frantic.

Awareness scales.

So does neglect.

The quiet work you do internally shapes the visible work you do externally.

Titles amplify patterns. They do not correct them.
I learned that later than I should have.

If you are a founder, your discipline becomes pace.
If you are a CEO, your clarity becomes direction.
If you are a board member, your steadiness becomes

governance.
If you are a parent, your presence becomes inheritance.

You cannot outsource alignment.

You can delegate tasks.
You can distribute responsibility.
You cannot delegate awareness.

The most dangerous form of misalignment is the one that looks like progress.

Revenue rising.
Recognition increasing.
Expansion accelerating.

And something inside thinning.

This is not an argument against ambition.

Ambition built everything you are proud of.

But ambition without structure is expensive.

And the bill rarely arrives all at once.

It arrives in fragments.

Fatigue you normalize.
Conversations you shorten.
Signals you dismiss.
Habits you justify.

Balance is not a fixed state.

It is a practice of return.

Return to recovery.
Return to stillness.
Return to structure.
Return to honesty.
Return to growth that feels deliberate, not desperate.

You will drift again. That is human.

The work is not to prevent drift.

It is to notice sooner.

If these stories did anything, I hope they slowed you down just enough to ask:

What in my life feels steady — but hollow?
What in my leadership feels strong — but strained?
What am I postponing because I am afraid of what it might reveal?

Clarity rarely shouts.

It waits.

You do not need to rebuild everything.

You need to stop abandoning the part that is asking for care.

The world may measure what you build.

You will live inside how you built it.

The body that carried you.
The mind that processed pressure.
The relationships that absorbed strain.
The systems that either supported you — or silently cracked.

Long after outcomes are forgotten, you will still be standing inside the structure you created.

Build that structure deliberately.

Not loudly.

Not per-formatively.

Just steadily enough that you can remain inside it without needing to escape it.

That is the work.

It doesn't end here…

* * * * * * *

Success will continue to evolve.
Markets will shift.
Roles will change.
People will come and go.

What will remain constant is the condition in which you meet those changes.

Alignment is not visible from the outside. It does not announce itself. It is felt in the steadiness of your decisions, the clarity of your thinking, and the absence of quiet panic behind visible progress.

You may still build aggressively.
You may still expand, lead, scale, and pursue.
But the question that endures is simpler than ambition:

Is the structure beneath your success stable enough to hold it?

Because in the end, the world measures what you built. You live with how you built it.

That difference determines everything.

* * * * * * *

Verses Kindler Publication

Verses Kindler Publication

Reach us through our website -

https://www.verseskindlerpublication.com/

For more information visit our

Instagram or Facebook page.

9 789347 494413

Printed at Repro India Ltd.